D0653379

WITHDRAWN

THREE MORE MELODRAMAS

By the same author

THREE MELODRAMAS

IT GIVES ME GREAT PLEASURE

MAKE 'EM LAUGH

THE GOLDEN AGE OF MELODRAMA

THREE MORE MELODRAMAS

by

RICHARD DENNIS
MICHAEL KILGARRIFF
and
PETER VENTHAM

Introduced and edited by
MICHAEL KILGARRIFF

SAMUEL  FRENCH

LONDON
NEW YORK TORONTO SYDNEY HOLLYWOOD

SAMUEL FRENCH LTD, 26 SOUTHAMPTON STREET, STRAND, LONDON WC2 7JE, or their authorized agents, issue licences to amateurs to give performances of these plays on payment of a fee. **The fee must be paid and the licence obtained before a performance is given.**

Licences are issued subject to the understanding that it shall be made clear in all advertising matter that the audience will witness an amateur performance; and that the names of the authors of the plays shall be included on all announcements and on all programmes.

The royalty fee indicated below is subject to contract and subject to variation at the sole discretion of Samuel French Ltd.

Basic fee for each and every performance by amateurs of each of these plays in the British Isles — Code C

In theatres or halls seating 600 or more the fee will be subject to negotiation.

In territories overseas the fee quoted above may not apply. Application must be made to our local authorized agents, or if there is no such agent, to Samuel French Ltd, London.

ISBN 0 573 00019 0

MADE AND PRINTED IN GREAT BRITAIN BY
LATIMER TREND & COMPANY LTD PLYMOUTH
MADE IN ENGLAND

CONTENTS

PREFACE

The success of my previous *Three Melodramas* has prompted me to offer herein three more sketches of the same genre especially designed for inclusion in revue, concert party, or more particularly Old Time Music Hall.

For the first I contacted Peter Ventham, with whom I had appeared in panto in Liverpool many years ago, and who during the run produced a very funny potted melodrama for a charity matinée at the Philharmonic Hall. This sketch, *Set A Thief To Catch A Thief*, had originally been written by Peter's father—himself a comic in the heyday of Variety. And so, although the version given here is considerably revised, the provenance of this playlet is impeccable.

My old friend and partner, Richard "Johnny" Dennis, and I had long mulled over the notion of a burlesque on Irving's most famous role, Mathias in *The Bells*. The resultant travesty is dedicated to his shade in affectionate respect.

Black-Eye'd Susan is founded in a long-standing admiration for this finest of all nineteenth-century nautical plays. I have telescoped (or perhaps I should say "collapsed") the plot, but the marine metaphors with which the original dialogue abounds scarcely needed any exaggeration.

Finally, these three pieces have each been tried and tested in performance. For the artistes they provide scope for broad but imaginative playing; for the audience they provide divers opportunities for participation and—of course—laughter.

MICHAEL KILGARRIFF

July 1973

INTRODUCTION

Melodrama is nothing if not predictable; it was this very attribute which offered 19th-century audiences some respite from as oppressive a mode of life as a nominally free society could devise. In the Never-Never Land of Melodrama people were honest and brave and truthful and patriotic; they believed in God and never went to the lavatory. And of course the goodies were, very naturally, white, Anglo-Saxon and Protestant. The non-Caucasian did occasionally make an appearance, but only as a faithful servant or chocolate-coloured buffoon. The villains were lying, cowardly, dishonest, blasphemous, lecherous blackguards without any redeeming feature whatsoever—foreigners were regarded in much the same light—and their reliably forthcoming downfalls could be savoured without any namby-pamby, wishy-washy feelings of pity or compassion.

Innocence in young females was so highly prized that many a poor girl went to her bridal-chamber so unprepared for the demands to be made on her that the revelation of her contractual obligations sent her clean off her pretty little head. Others, Nature being the hussy she is, might take to coition as the proverbial duck to water, and then, intoxicated with this new-found appreciation of What Life Had To Offer, begin to look askance at the smug, opinionated, hirsute Turk whom convention demanded should be her sole partner in the fleshly pleasures—and weep. "I was never told the truth about anything, I assure you," says Isabel, in Celia Dale's novel *Act Of Love*; "I might have tried to order things differently if I had." But she is trapped, hog-tied and incarcerated in the dungeon of respectability. Her youth passes, her life's course is fixed, and only the vicarious thrills of the melodrama can offer her a taste of what might have been.

But Papa's life was not so dull by any means, what with his clubs and his brandy, his cosy little love-nest in St John's Wood and his shrewd wheeling-and-dealing in the City. He also enjoyed the melodrama, though—while it was still fashionable. The qualities of chastity and honesty (in others) he approved of and was pleased to see them publicly propounded, even by persons who until 1824 were still statutory rogues and vagabonds.

Fashion percolates down through the social strata (although perhaps today the reverse is the case) and so early in the 19th century we find the labouring and bourgeois classes espousing all the repressive attitudes of their betters. By the time melodrama had been abandoned by the *haut-ton*, the *hoi polloi* was hooked and stayed faithful to the end—which can, I suppose, be taken as the start of the Great War.

Humour in melodrama is very unattractive as well as unfunny. While we can regard the execrable habit of punning as a harmless if tiresome fad, it is not so easy to accept the jokes which show the British character at its wilful worst, with its racial prejudice, rock-hard insularity, blind chauvinism, and a servile, cringing, cap-touching, forelock-tugging respect for the Table of Precedence.

The hero might or might not be a sprig of the nobility—it rather depended on the location of the theatre for which the piece was intended or the novel from which it had been culled. He will, of course, have an "educated" accent if the plot requires him to be revealed in the final scene as the Earl of Mummerset—"this locket proves your claim to the Mummerset millions, my lord!" To end up not only with the girl and a rich estate but a coronet as well was unquestionably the happiest ending imaginable. Alternatively if the hero was presented as an honest artisan he will be permitted a slight accent in order to highlight his loyalty to authority and devotion to duty—the very qualities on which Britain's greatness (i.e. Imperialism) was founded.

Even melodrama's villains were snobbily drawn. A villain must have wealth, power and influence to make him all the more dangerous to Honest Joe the plumber's mate. It was inconceivable that a fellow plumber's mate or even a fully time-served plumber could aspire to the eminence of villainy. Dear me, no—a villain is a person of consequence, *ergo* he must be of gentle birth, even if his actions are as remote from gentility as the stars up above. And in any case there will probably be a kindly old lord written in to show that the aristocracy's heart is fundamentally in the right place. Moreover, he may well turn out to be the heroine's long-lost father, which explains her posh accent[1]—she has little to do other than agonize, so she might as well do it nicely.

Were we then a nation of Uriah Heeps, outwardly humble and inwardly seething with bile and thoughts of revenge upon our masters? Unfortunately, the answer is no. We just didn't seem to care. We couldn't even aspire to the dignity of fatalism—we hadn't that much imagination. We just accepted that as God was an English gentleman (with escutcheon) and had created the Universe to His satisfaction, the pattern of life on this island was divinely ordained. To kick against the pricks was unpatriotic if not downright sacriligeous. So we blessed the squire and his relations and kept us in our proper stations. Rather than agitate for a revolution—or even a few mild reforms[2]—the 19th-century man in the street preferred to howl at Sweeney Todd or William Corder just as now our lives are dominated by football and the telly. We may grumble and inveigh against the duplicity of politicians and the bloody-mindedness of civil servants, but in our hearts we are still convinced that Britain is Best.

"But what opportunities those old plays gave to act! They were an actor's dream, allowing for full-range displays of personality and passion, unencumbered by subtleties of characterization or directors' quirks. The actor was king; he strode his stage with mighty strides, exuding a distillation of the finest virtue, the noblest sentiments—or the basest villainy, as the case may be—secure in the power of his technique and imagination to hold his audience rapt. What a chance for a pretty *ingénue* to display her daintiness and femininity; what a chance for a leading man to portray courage and resolution. Polish, grace, 'good address', a resonant speaking-voice—these were just as much part of an actor's equipment as fire and guts. And he was expected to sing, dance and tumble as well!" I quote the above[3] in defence of my

[1] I once appeared in a disgusting play called *The Opium Eaters* in which this creaky old device was used—and this play was written in the 1950's!

[2] The principal reformers (Howard, Ventham, Elizabeth Fry and the Quakers, Wilkes, Angela Burdett Coutts, Dickens, Cobden, Bright, Peel, Florence Nightingale) were all from the middle and mercantile classes. Not until the rise of Unionism was the working class able to have a say in its own destiny.

[3] From my own *Three Melodramas* (1969).

contention that it is wrong to burlesque melodrama today. The plays are quite ridiculous enough to a modern audience, so for players to burlesque is to gild the dandelion. English audiences especially love to discover humour for themselves; once it becomes apparent that the players are also finding the piece risible the whole exercise becomes sterile. As in farce the cast, while aware of the comedic possibilities of the piece, must appear to be in deadly earnest or all tension is dissipated.

Variety comics are notorious for their cavalier treatment of pantomime plot. Their neurotic compulsion to raise a laugh every ten seconds leads them to destroy the dramatic content of a pantomime—I once saw the funny half of a nationally-celebrated double act thrown down his script at the first morning's rehearsal and say, "We were engaged as comics not actors!" But actors in turn tend to treat melodrama with the same disrespect and refuse to take its situations seriously. Their professed dislike of corn is, I think, more a reluctance to sustain a full-blooded emotion, a fear of going over the top and appearing foolish. But life is full of challenges and a whole-hearted embrace of the grander passions is still marvellous theatre. Time and time again I have seen how "strong emotional playing has engendered a remarkably sympathetic response which even almost constant laughter has not entirely dissipated."[1]

Let us not therefore sell our melodrama short, for even in these three burlesques there are moments of truth which, if observed and cherished, will highlight the comedy besides offering a modicum of dramatic tension as a bonus.

So don't let your artistes regard the enterprise as a mere romp, and be more intent on pleasing themselves than the paying customers. I suggest that pantomime playing is the style to aim for—broad but not crude, obvious but not insensitive. The characters are only cyphers, perhaps, but even a cypher can have a heart.

As a general rule all dialogue should be played out front. Indeed, direct address to the audience is today in vogue. Peter Nicol's *National Health*, *A Day In The Death Of Joe Egg* and *Forget-Me-Not Lane* all delighted critics and audiences with the use of what they were pleased to call "music-hall" techniques, but which I would simply describe as "asides". Your players will find this difficult at first, but they should be encouraged to per-

[1] From my own *Three Melodramas* (1969).

severe, to hand out information to the audience rather than converse with each other.

The lines should moreover be delivered with speed and clarity, making each step in the plot crystal clear (amateurs especially tend either to be woefully slow or to gabble incoherently); business and gags must be orchestrated so that your audience is only asked to look at one place and one event at a time.

Finally, may I repeat that sincerity is of paramount importance: if the spectators become aware that your dramatis personae are finding the piece as ludicrous as they do themselves the whole undertaking is set at naught.

NOTES TO THE PRODUCER

Set A Thief To Catch A Thief by Peter Ventham & Michael Kilgarriff

Running time 15 minutes approx.

Your strongest and most experienced comic must be let loose on Alf. I would suggest that he speak in the local accent, with his dialogue altered to accommodate regional variations. The player should regard him as an Alf Garnett or Andy Capp, but he must also ooze charm or the constant interruptions may become too aggressive and alienating. Nor must he be allowed to run away with this sketch; don't let him insert too much of his own material or the piece will become tedious. The gags given here are known to work and to be of just the right number—if there are a string of additions the law of diminishing returns will soon begin to apply. In short, Alf's rumbustiousness must be controlled.

Charlie should be played in complete contrast, being distinctly short on grey matter. He responds very well to all Alf's witticisms, which are mostly directed at him.

Polly should be attractive and—horrid word—winsome. The poor girl has a thankless role, what with Alf's interjections and a criminally-inclined husband. But at least she has a happy ending to look forward to, and these parts can always be rescued from insipidity by a fresh and dainty young actress, brightly costumed. Her moves should be balletic; she goes from pose to pretty pose, presenting a picture of femininity at all times.

Peter is basically a good egg; he is the product of a minor public school who has had some bad luck, and who, in a momentary weakness, has strayed from the straight and narrow. But he can still show some sterling qualities, if he tries hard.

The Inspector (who should be doubled by the Chairman) has a slight Cockney accent. His manner will suggest P.C. Plod with a dash of sly venality, but he shouldn't be too slow. He will not take part in the final call.

Uncle Silas is a querulous old man, all a-tremble as he discovers his long-lost nephew. At the recognition scene both he and Peter will be bathed in tears. If your company is short of men and your Uncle Silas is willing to double, he can also play the Stage-Manager. If you are overloaded with men give one of them this brief but satisfying role—but he will not appear in any of the calls.

No set is necessary: the table and a chair (plus, of course, the hand props) are the only essentials. If you wish to elaborate, a small box interior with practical doors R and L can be designed to represent a humble living-room, with an aspidistra painted on the wall, together with painted windows, family portraits, hat-stand, fireplace, etc.

The precise staging of Alf's and Charlie's first entrance depends on the geography of the hall or theatre in which you will be performing; as indicated in the text this can be altered to suit.

Give your pianist a copy of the sketch from the first rehearsal, for background music should commence on Polly's first entrance and continue virtually non-stop until Peter's speech of thanks to the audience.

Alf's line "Oh, I've got kidney trouble, too," is a very big laugh, so Peter must on no account kill it by coming in too soon.

The cast should stoically ignore the interruptions (apart from waiting for laughs!) except where specifically indicated in the text.

In the final Black-Out Charlie and Alf should disappear without further gags or business, taking their box and beer-bottles with them.

If you have follow-spots they can pick up Alf and Charlie in the auditorium as they make their presence felt, and one spot should cover the two comics throughout. Apart from the two Black-Outs there need be no lighting changes.

The Bells by Richard Dennis & Michael Kilgarriff

Running time 10 minutes approx.

"Collapse of stout party" ran the caption of the famous *Punch* cartoon, and it is the collapse of Sir Henry Ermine's stout but unavailing efforts at dramatic validity which produce the laughs in this parody—but only if Sir Henry is immensely dignified, indomitably agonised and scrupulously sincere. This is not the place to dilate upon the nature of Comedy (far more learned pens than mine have attempted this without significant success) but all pundits agree that, as in tragedy, the essence of the beast is conflict.

And Conflict is certainly evident a-plenty in *The Bells*, which features the time-honoured notion of the earnest performer being sabotaged by incompetent stage-management. It is absolutely necessary therefore that your Sir Henry plays with the utmost integrity, since the comedy is derived, as I have said, almost entirely from the puncturing of his passionate endeavours.

His dramatic pretensions are in no way assisted by Ann and Christian, who should be physically quite unsuited to their roles, the intention being to demonstrate that, having been given a glowing encomium by the Chairman, the renowned Lyceum Company is clearly second-rate. Ann will be "refained" and more than somewhat *passée*; Christian should be stiff and awkward—he is not only a very poor player but is also plainly terrified of both the occasion and his fiancée. Again, however, both will try very hard.

But your leading-man should be presented as a good actor foiled at every turn by fools and incompetents. There is even an element of pathos in the spectacle of a great man of the theatre reduced to appearing in such a deplorable shambles, although this is not a quality to be dwelled upon. If it emerges, well and good, but don't try for it.

Sir Henry's desperation at the inadequacies of his fellow-artistes and the stage-management should be grafted on to Mathias' spiritual torment. We should be able to see in his performance these two elements quite clearly, at times separately and at times in combination. In other words the player will be acting two roles at once—Sir Henry *and* Sir Henry as Mathias. This is no mean challenge, and the difficulties of making the most of the role should not be underestimated.

He will always speak the word "my" as "me" (as did Irving himself), and although his diction, style of delivery and deportment will be studied and old-fashioned he must not rant too ponderously or become too hammy—remember he is a *good* actor. We must be able to appreciate that, given half a chance, he could well turn in a very thrilling performance indeed, just as I fully believe Irving would today. His movements will be economical and graceful, his personality mesmeric, and his authority total. Your most experienced leading man will not be wasted in this role, and he must be firmly restrained from guying the character.

Don't forget to encourage your actors to play out front.

Since Mathias (pronounced Ma'-tias) says that the victim of twenty years before was a Jew (the title of the French original of this play was *Le Juif Polonais*) I have given the Stage-Manager an exaggerated Cockney-Jewish accent. But if it is felt that this might give offence to your audience—a danger which can be avoided by casting a Jewish actor in the role—he can speak in the local regional dialect with his lines altered to suit. He should not be entirely insensitive to the demands of his office; he does his level best—it is just unfortunate that his best is nowhere near good enough.

The offstage sound effects can be varied according to equipment available and your budget. Only the sleigh bells, obtainable from musical instrument shops and toy shops, are essential. It is as well to have your effects at all rehearsals since they must be timed carefully to avoid a messy confusion. It will need two people to work them: the Stage-Manager himself and the unseen Morrie (who can, if necessary, be the Chairman).

The snow can be a quarter-bucketful of heat-insulating granules, a material which can be easily and quickly swept up for further use. The dust in the lime kiln can be a layer of talcum powder spread on a piece of stiff paper or cardboard and simply blown over Mathias on cue. The wind is most easily managed by use of an effects record, or, more crudely, by the Stage-Manager making an appropriate noise vocally.

The Chairman should be aware that in his introduction the word "Thespian", if given sufficient emphasis, gets a good positive reaction. Don't ask me why, I can only tell you that this is my experience.

As with all melodramas, music should start on cue and continue virtually without ceasing until the final Black-Out when it should stop abruptly in mid-bar. For instance, Ann will need a snatch of Mendelssohn's *Spring Song* on ". . . my heart is as light as thistledown . . ."; Christian will need the March from Wagner's *Tannhauser* for his entrance, and Mathias will require a triumphant fanfare for his.

Watch that the laugh on the first wrong sound effect—the motor horn—does not swamp the rattle and swanee whistle. Each wrong effect gets its own laugh, so they must be paced out accordingly.

If the "wrong" lighting cues are impracticable, simply cut the line ". . . and the moon shines its frosty radiance on the scene . . .".

The blundering attempts of Ann, Christian and the Stage-Manager to aid Mathias at the end must be carefully set and rehearsed so that the sequence of events is quite clearly defined. A couple of old blankets on the floor of your rehearsal room will be appreciated by the cast.

Black-Eye'd Susan by Michael Kilgarriff

Running time 15 minutes approx.

Although it was not the first, Douglas Jerrold's *Black-Eye'd Susan* was far and away the most successful of all the dozens of nautical melodramas written in the first half of the 19th century. It was originally produced at the Surrey Theatre in 1829, and ran for over 300 performances—an amazing run, since no play until that time had achieved even half that figure. The piece was constantly revived throughout the century and attracted numerous imitations and burlesques. The original William was T. P. Cooke, himself a naval hero of the Napoleonic Wars, who usually appeared sporting his campaign medal. (Jerrold had also served before the mast as a boy.)

Cooke played William until the end of his career at the age of seventy, and was "the best sailor out of all sight and hearing that ever trod the stage". His hornpipe and cutlass work were especially commended by all who saw him, and he evidently presented William as the archetypal Jolly Jack Tar, all swashbuckling manliness and rectitude. This, then, must be the model for your William; the slightest hint of parody must be ruthlessly quashed, since to our ears his sentiments and mode of expression are more than sufficiently quaint. There is no percentage in burlesquing a burlesque.

Much more can be gleaned from this sketch than may appear. I like to think that the charm and engaging simplicity of the original have not been totally destroyed in this version, so encourage your romantic juveniles to play as realistically as they can—as I have said in my preamble a touch of genuine passion will help to highlight the absurdities and give your audience a little more than they bargained for, which is always a pleasant surprise.

Susan must of course have dark eyes (believe it or not, I once saw a Susan with bright blue eyes!) and should be played with spirit. Her joy and relief at William's return sends her into floods of tears; when she thinks she is about to lose him again her passion knows no bounds. But she must not be slow—it is a common error to imagine that strong emotions can only be expressed at tortoise-pace.

The Captain is the traditional villain, but, true to the age, a King's officer and a gentleman could not be shown to be wholly bad, and so he rescues William in the customary nick of time. Doggrass must be contrasted by being played as a combination of Ebenezer Scrooge and Uriah Heep. The Admiral, as played by the Chairman, will put on his eye-patch, epaulettes and hat during the fade and Black-Out at the end of Scene III.

The principal source of laughs are (i) the antique device of one man playing a multiplicity of roles, and (ii) William's constant use of nautical metaphor. Your Doggrass (etc.) should be one of the younger and more versatile character men in your company—I say younger since he has to work hard and fast. It is as well if he has an assistant in the wings R to hold the musket in Scene III and to help with the changes. The various disguises should not be too complete or he will not be recognized, thus nullifying his efforts.

The location of this sketch is a port in Kent, so your front cloth, if you have one, will be a gaily painted quayside scene. Also the accents of Doggrass, William and Susan will be faintly rural.

If the Chairman stresses "th*ugg*ery, skul*dugg*ery" and then gives a minute pause on "and bu . . caneering" he will be rewarded by a loud, long laugh. In her scenes with Doggrass, Susan will not react to his bad breath—this business would be far too coarse for a heroine to indulge in; she can, however, give the tiniest of reactions when she is clinging to William in Scene III and he says, "Aye, Susan, it's hard . . .". The picture-on-the-wall gag is optional, but if you can run to a box-interior it is worth the laugh. William must be on his guard for a laugh on "I'll be pooped!" If this occurs he should stop and repeat the line from the beginning—and if he says the line straight out front it *will* get a laugh. William can also take on his own podium at the start of the Court Martial scene. Pike can be played as a limp-wristed effeminate, if preferred.

* * *

The songs included in the text are available at the back of the copy. Your pianist, if given a copy of the text from early rehearsals, can ad lib. a running accompaniment in the style of the silent cinema days.

SET A THIEF TO CATCH A THIEF

This version was first produced at the Dunes Theatre, Mablethorpe, on 27th May 1973, with the following cast:

Chairman	Mr Brian Hewitt-Jones
Alf	Mr Frankie Murray
Charlie	Mr Stephen Price
Polly	Miss Debbie Young
Peter	Mr Andrew Sketchley
Inspector Hawkshaw	Mr Richard Avon
Uncle Silas	Mr Ken Costigan

Directed by Mr Brian Hewitt-Jones

Scene: A humble suburban living-room

CAST

Alf	A vulgar working-class person
Charlie	His simple-minded friend
Polly	All things nice
Peter	Polly's weak husband
Inspector Hawkshaw	Can be doubled by Chairman
Uncle Silas	A troubled old man

(There is also a **Stage-Manager** who need not in fact appear; or he can be doubled by **Uncle Silas**)

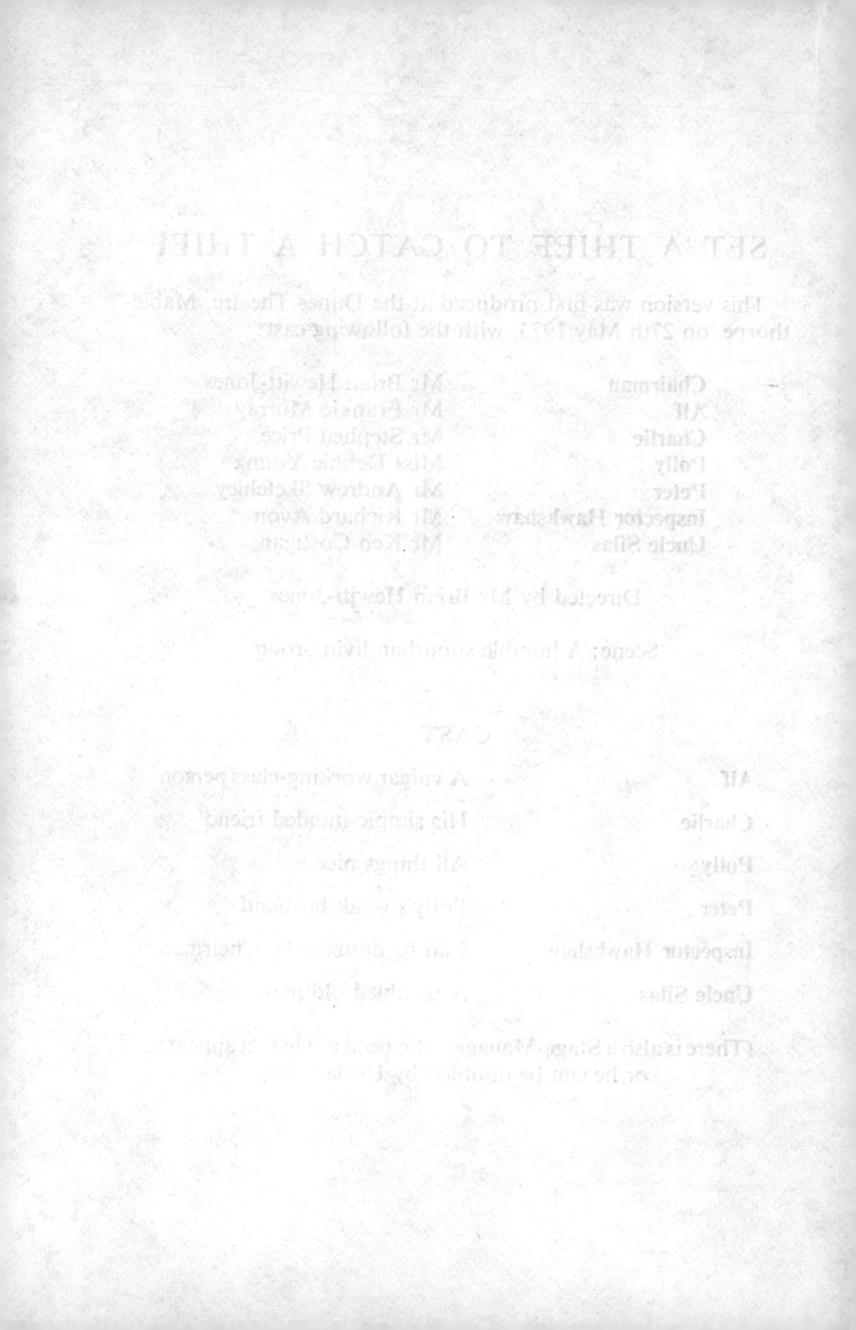

SET A THIEF TO CATCH A THIEF

(*All moves are given under the presumption that the Chairman's table is down* R)

Chairman Prepare now, Ladies and Gentlemen, for your withers to be wrung . . . (*To a woman in the audience*) Have you ever had your withers wrung, dear? . . . No, well, you need to be fit, don't you . . . as we proudly present our *Thespian* interlude, entitled *Set A Thief To Catch A Thief*, brought to you tonight at *enormous expense*, and——

Alf (*coming down the prompt side aisle of the auditorium*) Hello, Harry—this should be good if it lasts . . .Hello, Missus! Where's your old man, then? You want to keep an eye on him, you know . . . (*To the Chairman*) Carry on, old son . . . Enjoying yourself, George? They say the comic's good (*or a well-known member of the cast*) when he's sober . . . (*To the Chairman again*) All right, Squire, don't let me interrupt you . . . Wotcher, Teddy—I see you've got the wife with you. Oh, no, it's not the wife, she's got a box of chocolates . . . (*By now he is down at the front*)

Chairman (*who has vainly been trying to carry on*) —brought to you tonight, as I was saying, at *enormous expense* . . .

Alf (*to Chairman*) 'Ere, 'ave you seen my pal, Charlie? Charlie? Char . . . !

Charlie (*coming down the* OP *aisle*) 'Ere I am, Alf! Over 'ere!

Alf Where 'ave you been?

Charlie Outside waiting for you. Excuse me. (*He pushes his way along a row*)

Alf Where?

Charlie Outside waiting for you . . .

Alf I can't hear a blind word you're saying . . . (*To Chairman who again has been vainly trying to speak*) Shut up, will you? (*To Charlie again*) Now, where've you been?

Charlie Outside waiting for you, Alf.

Alf I told you inside. Daft as a brush. (*Producing two bottles of beer*) Have you got the opener?

Chairman Let's have a little order, please!

Alf That's very civil—two more of these, thanks very much.

Chairman Do you know you can be arrested for annoying people?

Alf You should know anyway.

Chairman Will you kindly sit down?

Alf What—with this common lot? Not likely—I've got a ticket for a box.

Chairman I'm afraid we don't have any boxes in this theatre.

Alf No boxes? I've been done! I'm not sitting down here with this riff-raff—dunno what you might pick up. Look at that! (*He picks up an imaginary flea from a person in the audience and stamps on it*) Worse than our ginger tom . . .

Chairman I tell you we don't have any boxes.

Alf I've paid for a box and I want a box!

Chairman Oh, very well—anything to keep you quiet. (*He calls to the wings* L) Have we a box, please?

A box or beer crate is hurled on to the stage from down L*; or, if the Stage-Manager is to be seen, a bedraggled, curmudgeonly figure shambles on stage muttering oaths under his breath. He slams the box down with a vicious look at the Chairman and exits* L

Note: If the theatre does possess a box, Alf can appear in it from the start of the sketch. Charlie will enter as indicated and after the line "You should know anyway" can clamber into the box assisted by Alf with ad lib. lines such as "Come on, Charlie, up you come, lad," "This isn't doing my hernia any good," etc. etc. All the following lines and business about the box will of course be omitted. The flea gag can be transferred to the box, with Alf finding it on the plush curtains perhaps. The geography of the auditorium will determine how Alf's and Charlie's entries can best be arranged.

The Chairman sets the box down L *below the tab-track; Alf and Charlie ascend to the stage and sit on it, with Alf on the right*

Chairman There you are, Gentlemen.

Alf That's better. Come on, Charlie. Where's that ruddy opener? My throat's like a gorilla's armpit.

Charlie opens his shirt and begins to pull out a long string tied round his neck

What's all this? You searching for buried treasure or something?

At last, with a squeak or two, Charlie gets out the opener and hands it to Alf

Blimey—it's still warm! (*He opens the two bottles, handing one to Charlie. Then to the Chairman*) Get on with it, then!
Chairman Open the curtains, please!
Alf (*to Charlie who is putting the opener back*) Stop fidgeting!

The curtains open to reveal a rudimentary interior set with doors R *and* L *and a table up* C

Chairman And now, Ladies and Gentlemen, I want you to imagine that what you see is the interior of a working girl's home.
Alf Looks like she's had the bailiffs in.
Chairman (*calling to the wings* L) Now I want three chairs, please.
Alf Hooray! Hooray! Hooray!

Charlie joins in

Chairman Three *chairs*, please.

A single chair is hurled on and a voice from off stage L *shouts "That's all we've got . . . !" or the surly Stage-Manager can appear and slam a chair down, mutter the line viciously and stalk off* L. *If the latter, Alf can say "He enjoys his work, doesn't he . . . ?"*

Alf I said they'd had the bailiffs in . . .
Chairman (*setting the chair by the* L *of the table; embarrassed*) Ha, ha, ha . . . now then: on my right is the girl's bedroom——

Charlie rises immediately and takes a couple of steps towards the bedroom but is pulled back by Alf

Alf Down, boy! Down!
Chairman —and on my left——

Alf —at fourteen stone eight and a half pounds——
Chairman (*ignoring Alf*) —the door to the street.
Alf Is that all?
Chairman (*exasperated*) Yes!
Alf Where's the how's-yer-father then?
Chairman (*ignoring him loftily*) And now, with your kind indulgence——
Alf What a crawler . . .
Chairman —we proudly present our dramatic sketch *Set A Thief To Catch A Thief*. Thank you.

The Chairman begins to exit L

Alf What are you thanking us for—you haven't done anything yet!

The Chairman exits L, *giving a hard look at Alf*

'Evening—(*after the Chairman has gone*)—I thought he'd never go.

Plaintive music. Enter Polly L *carrying a baby*

Hello, sweetheart! See you after? I've got me tandem . . .
Polly (*centre*) How cold the night is . . .
Alf She hasn't paid the coalman.
Polly And I am all alone.
Alf You will be after this performance. I've seen a better turn in my mother-in-law's eye.
Polly My Peter has been away for three years. I wonder what he has been doing?
Alf Three years. He's in the Scrubs, I bet you—wonder if the food's improved?
Polly I wonder why he doesn't write?
Alf No lead in his pencil!
Polly Why doesn't he return? I'm so lonely . . . (*She moves* R, *sobbing*)
Alf The lodger must be away, too.
Polly And what about my little flesh and blood? (*Indicating the baby*)

Alf Aye, aye! The plot thickens. (*To the audience*) She's certainly been hatching something.
Polly My little one . . . two years old today.
Alf How much?
Polly (*involuntarily replying*) Two years old today.
Alf How long's your husband been away?
Polly Three years—oh! (*Realizing*) My little one . . . *four* years old today.
Alf Four? Must be a midget!
Polly I must go and put the little tot in his cot.
Alf Or on his pot.

Polly exits R

Knock on the door L

(*Calling*) There's someone at the door, love . . . (*More knocks*) I say, there's someone at the door—(*third set of knocks*)—there's someone at the bloody door!

Enter Polly R

Polly Ah! I thought I heard a knock at the blo—at the door.
Alf Deaf as a post . . .

Enter Peter shabbily dressed

Polly (*running to him* LC) Dearest!

They embrace

Alf If that's the coalman she'll soon have plenty of slack in her bunker.
Polly Peter!
Peter Polly!

They embrace again

Alf (*to Charlie*) Clarence!
Charlie Ermyntrude!

They rise and embrace

Polly I thought that you were dead, but now that you've kissed me . . .
Alf She knows he's dead.

Alf and Charlie sit

Peter (*crossing to* RC) Polly . . .
Polly Yes, Peter?
Peter I have a confession to make.
Alf (*to the audience*) This is it—this is where you cry your eyes out.
Polly (*crossing to Peter*) Spare me nothing, dearest.
Alf Careful, this is a family show. If you come from that sort of family . . .
Peter (*crossing down* L) Polly, I—I——
Polly Yes, Peter?
Peter —I—er—I——
Alf Come on, they shut at ten-thirty.
Peter —I—haven't been true to you.
Alf You dirty dog!
Polly Untrue to me? Oh, Peter, how could you? You, with your innocent face . . .
Alf What—that mush? She wants specs.
Polly How came you to have such trusting eyes?
Alf They came with the body.
Peter I haven't been playing the straight game. (*Moving up to chair* L *of the table*) I've been out with the boys.
Alf Hello! You can't fight that, gal.
Peter (*sitting*) Gambling every morning, horse-racing every afternoon . . .
Alf Snakes and ladders every evening . . .
Peter For three nights now I have tramped the streets, mile after mile, footsore and weary—what else could I do?
Alf Buy a bike!
Peter Oh, Polly, I am ruined! Disgraced! (*He sobs over the table*)
Polly (*to* R *of the table*) Then what have we to look forward to in our married life?
Alf He's only been away three years and she's forgotten already!
Polly (*running round to Peter's left and kneeling by his side*) Oh,

my dear, let us forget the past, then we can be blissfully happy. (*Taking his left hand*)

Peter (*wallowing in self-pity. Pulling his hand away*) Nay, 'twill never be thus—'twill never be thus!

Alf 'Twon't if he twalks like a twit!

Peter (*to Alf*) Will you please be quiet? I appeal to you!

Alf You don't appeal to me in the slightest, mate! . . . I'm not one of your boys . . . go on, get on with it while you're here.

Polly Tell me more, Peter—I must have it all. (*Rising*)

Alf Cor—she hasn't forgotten . . .

Peter (*turning to her on the chair*) Oh, Polly. I—I—I . . .

Alf Has he got hiccups or something?

Peter Polly, I've—stolen a wallet. (*He produces it and places it on the table*)

Alf He's a tea-leaf!

Polly (*breaking away* L) Whatever made you do that?

Peter (*rising and moving* RC) I wanted money! I wanted love, life and laughter!

Alf (*getting out a cigarette*) You should have tried Hackney Marshes! (*Or local slum area, name of a big firm, abattoir, crematorium or similar*)

Polly Where did you get that wallet?

Charlie gets out matches and lights one for Alf

Peter I saw it sticking out of an old man's pocket.

Alf Where did you expect to see it? Sticking out of his—(*sees the lighted match*)—ah, thanks . . .

Peter (*crossing to Polly* LC) I have been followed—the police are after me.

Heavy footfalls are heard off L

That sounds like the Inspector!

Alf Sounds like he's got a wooden leg.

Peter Where shall I hide?

Polly Yonder—in the bedroom.

Peter Yes!

Peter runs and exits R

Alf Remember the way, do you?

Enter the Inspector, who can be the Chairman with a moustache, cloak and top hat

Inspector I am Detective Inspector Hawkshaw of the Yard.
Alf The back yard, I should think.
Inspector Well, you know what I have come for . . .
Alf You'll have to wait your turn. (*Pointing to the bedroom*) It's engaged.
Polly (*moving to his right*) Oh, please, Inspector . . .
Inspector Out of my way, woman. (*He pushes her aside. Crosses to* RC, *starts and turns back to the table*) What's this? A wallet? (*He goes to the table and picks it up*)
Alf (*slapping his knee*) God that was quick!
Inspector The criminal cannot be far away . . . (*He looks significantly at the door* R)
Alf Won't be long now. He'll whip out his truncheon any second, you watch.

The Inspector moves purposefully to the door R

Polly (*running across and kneeling by his side*) Oh, no, Inspector! Don't take him away, please! (*Taking his left hand*) I'll do anything!
Inspector (*out front*) Anything . . . ?

Alf and Charlie chortle and rub their hands with gleeful anticipation

Polly (*innocently*) Anything . . . !
Inspector (*after a brief struggle with his conscience*) No! (*Extricating his hand*) Duty comes first!
Alf What a mug!

Polly rises and moves to up RC, *disconsolately*

Inspector (*calling through the door* R) Show yourself, miscreant! (*Flexing his knees*) There is no way out!

There is the sound of ripping material

Alf There is now!

Enter Peter woefully

Peter All is lost!
Inspector Aha! (*Crossing to the door* L) Now then—will you come in, sir?

Enter Uncle Silas who can be the Stage-Manager with a large moustache. He stands on the Inspector's left

Alf Who's this? Lord Kitchener? Hello, Dad . . .
Inspector Tell me, sir—is this the man who took your wallet?
Silas (*crossing Inspector to* C *and Peering short-sightedly*) Yes, Inspector . . . (*He starts, peers harder and starts again with little expostulations of amazement*)
Alf He's got D.T.'s . . .
Silas Peter!

Peter also starts, peers closely at Silas and similarly goes into a welter of amazement

Alf They've all got it!
Peter Uncle Silas!

They embrace C. *Polly moves down* R

Silas My boy! My boy! At last my search is over! For twenty years my conscience has given me no rest, ever since I cheated you out of your inheritance when you were but a little lad!
Alf (*in disgust at this hackneyed turn of plot*) Oh, no . . .
Silas (*taking a wallet from the Inspector and handing it to Peter*) Keep the wallet—it is rightfully thine. In it you will find the title deeds of your estate and papers which prove that you are the Earl of Ealing. (*Or local*)
Peter Polly! I am a peer! (*They embrace joyfully*)
Alf Oh, I've got kidney trouble, too . . . !
Peter (*crossing to the Inspector*) Take this for your trouble, Inspector. (*He takes a note from the wallet and hands it to the Inspector*)
Inspector Oh, thanks very much, sir . . . (*Taking it*)
Alf Look at that! You can tell he's not a (*local*) copper . . .

The Inspector coughs and rubs the fingers of his right hand to indicate that a little more is required. Peter gives him another note

Alf Oh, I don't know, though . . .

Inspector Thank you, sir. (*Touching his hat*) Good night, all.

The Inspector exits L

Peter Well, that only goes to show, Polly.
Polly (*crossing to him so that they are both* C) What is that, dearest Peter?
Peter You can lead a horse to the water . . . (*This is said out front, straight to the audience*)
Alf But your rhubarb must be forced!

Black-Out. Tabs close. Lights up and Tabs open to disclose a picture: Peter has Polly in a Valentino-like embrace, Silas, R, *is gazing at them fondly, the Inspector is leering in through the door* L.

Tabs. The second call is a straight line-up. As the cast is taking its bows Alf and Charlie are cheering and applauding noisily and a touch derisively

Peter Thank you, Ladies and Gentlemen . . .

Alf and Charlie continue

Thank you—thank you—(*to them*)—*QUIET!*

There is a stunned pause

Alf (*to Charlie*) Was he shouting at you?
Charlie No.
Alf (*indicating the audience*) It must have been that lot down there. I said they were common . . .
Peter (*pressing on*) On behalf of my supporting artistes, I would like to thank you very much for the way you—(*glaring at Alf and Charlie*)—or most of you——
Alf Nasty, nasty . . .
Peter —have received our little drama this evening.
Alf Drama? I thought it was a farce.
Peter And you will be pleased to know that as a result of your heart-warming applause——
Alf They were just trying to keep their hands warm.
Peter (*getting angry again*) —we have been asked to extend the run of this play for a further two weeks——
Alf Never!

Peter (*biting on the bullet*) —and, furthermore, I would like to add that I myself will be appearing in the same role.
Alf You will?
Peter (*furious*) Yes, I will!
Alf Oh, no, you won't! (*He produces a revolver and shoots Peter*)

Black-Out. No further calls. Tabs in. Lights up as the Chairman reappears as himself—he need not have been in the final line-up in order to divest himself of hat, cloak, moustache, etc

THE BELLS

This version was first produced at the Pindar of Wakefield, Gray's Inn Road, London, W.C.1, for the Aba Daba Music Hall on Friday, 9th March 1973, with the following cast:

Chairman	Mr Michael Kilgarriff
Sir Henry Ermine	Mr Johnny Dennis
Stage-Manager	Mr Norman Warwick
Ann	Miss Norma Dunbar
Christian	Mr David Ryder-Futcher

Director: Mr. Johnny Dennis

Scene: A village in Alsace

CAST

Ann	The daughter. She is by no means in the first flush of youth, and her figure can be said to be on the generous side.
Christian	Her fiancé. A pimply, gangling youth, with glasses—he should be played as though very short-sighted.
Mathias	Ann's father. The local innkeeper. A tragic figure in more ways than one. Played by Sir Henry Ermine.
The Stage-Manager	Surly and very Jewish

THE BELLS

(*All moves are given under the presumption that the Chairman's table is down* R)

Chairman (*moving to down* C) And now, Ladies and Gentlemen, following the tradition of this house in bringing you only the very finest artistes, it is with humble pride that I announce a matchless example of the Thespian art . . . Yes, here, gracing our unworthy stage with members of his celebrated company from the Lyceum Theatre, Stepney (*or local*), is none other than Sir Henry Ermine, to give us a seminal scene from his greatest triumph: *The Bells*. I would like to express . . .

Sir Henry (*appearing round up* L *entrance wearing a very long dressing-gown and with pince-nez*) Mr Chairman . . . Mr Chairman . . . !

Chairman (*disconcerted but sidling over to him*) Er, yes, Sir Henry?

Sir Henry Is your Stage-Manager fully cognizant of his duties?

Chairman I assure you, Sir Henry, he is very experienced.

Sir Henry But are you sure he is reliable? His manner seems to me to be far too casual . . .

Stage-Manager (*appearing just on stage down* L, *smoking a cigar*) I heard that, moishe. You do your job and I'll do mine. Don't you worry about me . . . (*Exiting*) My life! (*There is a clink of bottles off stage*) Who put those there . . . ?

Chairman Don't worry, Sir Henry. I'm sure everything will be in order.

Sir Henry exits up L, *unconvinced, tripping over his dressing-gown*

(*Moving back to down* C) So now, Ladies and Gentlemen, I have the honour to announce Sir Henry Ermine and the Lyceum Company in a scene from Mr Leopold Lewis's famed drama: *The Bells!* (*He sits down* R)

Dramatic music. Lights lower. Music becomes lighter as Ann enters up L. *She enters opening an imaginary door. Loud wind is heard. She pushed the door shut and the wind cuts off immediately*

Ann (*coming down* C) My, what a dreadful night! The snow will fall so heavily at any moment! But despite the inclement weather my heart is light as thistledown,—(*she trips thunderously round the stage*)—for tomorrow—(*she pauses to catch her breath*)—for tomorrow I am to be wed to Christian, a lad from the village.

A quick snatch of "The Wedding March" from the pianist

(*With a glare at the pit*) But the only sorrow to cloud my joy is the thought that I shall be leaving my dear, dear father on his own—for Mama has passed away . . . (*She brushes away a tear*) Hark—a footfall!

Christian opens an imaginary door up L *and again loud wind is heard. He pushes the door shut with an effort and again the wind cuts off immediately. He is covered in snow*

Christian (*with arms outstretched*) My love!

Ann also has her arms outstretched and balletically they join C *in a chaste embrace. Christian is all but smothered*

What a snowstorm! I have known many *in this region of Alsace*—(*this to be said straight out front, heavily imparting plot to the audience*)—but nothing to compare with this . . . Is your father returned?

Ann No, dearest Christian. He is still upon the road. (*Coyly*) We are alone.

Christian (*not too enthusiastically*) Good. (*He takes her in a Valentino-like embrace, but she is too heavy for him and they both almost tumble to the ground*)

Ann (*releasing herself*) No, no! You must not lay hand on me till we are wed on the morrow. Hark—another footfall! It must be my father!

She clears down L *and Christian clears down* R

The stage darkens except for a concentration of light on the up L *entrance. Music rises to a crescendo. Enter Mathias grandly*

Mathias 'Tis I!

The wind is very, very loud. Sir Henry holds an impressive pose, with one hand raised dramatically; in the other he holds a hat box. The Chairman rises and applauds, encouraging the audience to follow his lead. Sir Henry gravely takes a bow—it is his due, after all, though he looks a little startled at the force of the gale

Ann Father!

Mathias What a snow-storm! (*He turns to push the door shut and a bucketful of snow is thrown over him. Gamely he shuts the door with an effort but the wind continues unabated as he attempts to speak*) Heaven be—heaven be . . . (*Looking meaningfully at the down* L *corner*) I'll shut the door . . . ! (*He mimes shutting the door again. The wind stops*) Heaven be praised that I have returned 'ere nightfall. Ah, Christian . . . (*He makes a move to Christian down* R *and walks out of the follow-spot into darkness. He returns, looks at the operator and makes the move again slowly*) Ah, Christian, my boy . . . (*He puts his hand on Christian's shoulder heartily. Christian sinks*)

Christian Good evening, sir. I rejoice to see you safe.

Lights creep up to full

Mathias (*moving to* C *with heavy good humour*) Thank 'ee, thank 'ee, my boy. (*He starts to undo the clasp on his cloak with the hat box under his arm*)

Ann (*going to him*) Let me take your hat and cloak, Father. (*She whisks the hat off his head and takes the cloak too soon. It is still fastened round his neck and she almost pulls him over. Finally the clasp is undone and she takes the hat and cloak to the down* L *entrance. A hand comes out with one finger extended upon which she hangs the garments. The hand withdraws into the wings. Mathias and Christian chat together while this business is being completed*)

Mathias And look here, child. I have brought ye a gift! (*He proffers the box. Christian clears* R)

Ann (*running to Mathias's* L) What is it, Father?

Mathias (*chuckling avuncularly*) Open and see!

Ann Oh, how kind you are, Father! (*She goes* RC. *Christian holds the box while she opens it. Mathias clears down* LC *and strikes a smug pose. Ann takes out a hat which she obviously doesn't like*) Oh . . . how nice . . . Is it for me?

Mathias For whom else? Not for Christian, I fancy . . . ! (*He laughs heavily, but there is no response from the audience. His eyes move uneasily from side to side and he laughs even more heartily, looking at the Chairman who, embarrassed at the audience's lack of response, laughs noisily and indicates to the house that this is a joke and that it would be disrespectful not to laugh. Sir Henry is not pleased, but reassumes good humour like the great professional that he is*) It is for your wedding-day, dearest girl. You shall be the prettiest girl in the province!

Ann (*running to him and kissing his cheek*) How kind and thoughtful you are, Father mine. Come, Christian, let us tend to the horses and give them their oats.

Ann grabs Christian's hand and pulls him off up R. *He is obviously terrified of the imputation*

Mathias (*gazing fondly after them*) Dear children . . . (*To* C, *throwing himself into a dramatic pose as the lights lower, he gazes about wild-eyed*) Those bells . . . ! Curse 'em . . . ! After twenty years I still seem to hear the bells—(*obviously a sound effect has been missed*)—yes, after twenty years I still seem to hear the bells—(*still nothing, very deliberately*)—*the bells!*

Stage Man (*sidling round the down* L *wing holding a cue-sheet to the stage lights*) What was that again, moishe?

Mathias (*desperate*) I hear the bells!

Stage Man (*reading*) ". . . hear the bells . . ." Oh yeah . . . Morrie! (*Going off*) Give us the bells.

There is the sound of a motor horn, a rattle, then a swanee whistle

(*Reappearing briefly with the swanee whistle*) I wondered where that had got to. (*He blows it again as he goes off*)

Mathias (*raving*) I hear the bells!

Stage Man (*off*) All right, all right. (*A loud clink of bottles again and a muffled curse*) Ah, here we are . . . (*Sleigh bells are heard*) All right, squire. Carry on.

Mathias What is this jangling in my ears . . . ?

The bells are heard again

Stage Man (*off*) Good boy, Morrie. Spot on.
Mathias Why tonight? On the eve of my daughter's nuptials! Ah! Yes, of course—it is the very night . . . the anniversary of that fatal deed . . . the very hour . . . Ah! a sensation of giddiness seizes me . . . ! (*He staggers hammily down* L)

The Stage Manager appears with arms outstretched to catch him but Mathias staggers away to down C. *Exit the Stage Manager*

Shall I call for help?

Re-enter the Stage Manager

No . . .

Exit the Stage Manager, muttering

Have courage, Mathias. The Jew is dead!
Stage Man (*off*) Oi vey!
Mathias The dread scene haunts me still—(*he is now in a trance-like state*)—the Jew goes out of this door—(*wanders up* L) —taking his gold with him . . . He is gone . . . I shall follow him . . . Where is the axe? . . . The axe . . . !
(*As he goes back down* C, *glassy eyed, with claw-like hand reaching for an imaginary axe, the Stage Manager sidles on endeavouring to remain inconspicuous and holding a real axe which he tries to hand to Sir Henry. The great actor, however, has his back turned*) Ah, here it is! . . . (*The Stage Manager sees that Mathias has hold of nothing, shakes his head uncomprehendingly and sidles off down* L *again*) My sharp axe—(*he tests its edge*)—now—(*wandering in a large circle about the stage*)—I am on the road . . . How cold it is! (*He shivers*) Come, Mathias: you shall possess the gold—courage! . . . I follow him across the fields . . . kill a man . . . kill! . . . No! . . . *Yes!* You can pay off all your debts . . . your family will want for nothing . . . you will be rich . . . it must be, Mathias, that you will kill him! Ooooh, what a dreadful silence . . .

Clink of bottles off stage, followed by a loud "Shhh!" and "Sorry!" in a half-whisper from Morrie

Three o'clock strikes . . .

Three beats with a spoon on the base of a large saucepan are heard

And—(*another extraneous beat is sounded*)—and the moon shines its frosty radiance on the scene . . .

Either a short dead Black-Out, followed by "Sorry, Squire," from the Stage-Manager off L, *or a blue filter can be very slowly and noisily inserted into the follow-spot or a flood in the wings which comes on at this point*

Listen . . . the Jew approaches . . .

Enter the Stage-Manager

Get off, you fool!

Stage Man (*exiting down* L) He's meshuggah . . . !

Mathias The Jew approaches—I hear the sleigh bells!

Stage Man (*again entering down* L *with his cue-sheet*) Hold it . . . it's all go tonight . . . Let's have a butcher's . . . oh, yeah . . . (*Going off*) He wants that bell again, Morrie!

But again we hear the hooter and the rattle

(*Off*) No, son—the bells! The bleeding bells!

At last the sleigh bells are heard

Mathias The bells! The bells! I have you now, Jew. I have you now! (*He swings an imaginary axe. Off down* L. *There is a thud and a male scream*) Be quick, Mathias! Carry him to the lime kiln . . . to the lime kiln—(*mimes picking up a corpse and carrying it to the up* L *entrance*)—into the lime kiln—(*as he pushes the corpse off a cloud of dust envelopes him, making him cough and splutter. He recovers gamely, though*)—how heavy he was! —(*He is now down* C *again*)—What have I done? . . . (*Moving down* L) What have I done? Those eyes . . . staring at me! Oooh . . . they will find me, and try me . . . and find me guilty . . . and sentence me to hang! (*His hands are around his own neck in an agony of anticipation*) No! No! Take the rope from me neck! Take the rope from me neck! Aaagh!

Ann and Christian rush on up R

Ann Father! }
Christian Sir! } *Speaking together*

Simultaneously the Stage-Manager rushes on down L. *He, Ann and Christian run to Mathias's aid as he staggers down* C. *The would-be rescuers crash into each other and fall to the floor in a tangle*

Mathias (*clutching at his neck*) I'm choking . . . the rope . . . it's choking me!

Ann and Christian rise; also the Stage-Manager who takes a rope from his pocket

Stage Man Righto, my son. Anything to oblige . . . (*He swiftly loops the rope round Mathias's neck and pulls, garrotting him. Mathias's eyes bulge. Black-Out. Tabs in, if any*)

No calls

Chairman Thank you, Ladies and Gentlemen. We have been privileged to witness Sir Henry Ermine's farewell performance . . . and not before time . . . and now to continue the programme we proudly present, *etc.*

* * *

If the Chairman is helping with the sound effects, after "Don't worry, Sir Henry," he can say: "I will personally go behind the scenes to ensure that everything will be in order." And after making the final introduction he can do just that. This procedure is especially helpful for a stage which has no wings; the cast must be smuggled up to behind screens during the preceding interval.

BLACK-EYE'D SUSAN

This version was first produced at the Queen's Theatre, Hornchurch, on Tuesday, 14th November 1972, with the following cast:

Chairman/Admiral	Mr Kenneth Keeling
Susan	Miss Bronwen Williams
Captain Crosstree, R.N.	Mr Bernard Taylor
William	Mr Roy Desmond
Doggrass	
Seaweed	
Marine	
Quid	Mr Christopher Emmett
Pike	
Dame Hatley	

Directed by Mr Antony Carrick

Prologue—a quayside in a Kent port

Scene I	Susan's cottage
Scene II	As for the Prologue
Scene III	As for Scene I
Scene IV	The Admiral's cabin
Scene V	The quarterdeck

The time is summer, 1829

BLACK-EYE'D SUSAN

CAST

William	A Jolly Jack Tar	
Captain Crosstree	A Bold, Bad Captain, R.N.	
Susan	William's young wife	
Admiral	Stern but just	
Doggrass	Susan's Uncle, but a scurvy knave	To be played by one actor
Seaweed	William's Irish/Scots/ Welsh shipmate	
Marine	Only Obeying Orders	
Quid	A Jewish seaman	
Pike	A Lancashire seaman; or an effeminate sea-man; or both	
Dame Hatley	Susan's aged companion while William is at sea	

Settings: Little or none. A chair up LC for Susan to collapse into; a small twelve-inch rostrum for William to stand on to be hanged; use may also be made of the Chairman's table and chair, which in this script are taken as down L.

If available a front cloth may be used—ideally a suitably painted roller cloth (see Richard Southern's *Changeable Scenery* (1951) p. 172); for the final scene the ship's deck can be suggested by flying in some rat-lines and sliding off any interior flats to reveal the sky-cloth or cyclorama.

For this sketch, however, no elaborations of scenery or lighting are required—although if the facilities of tabs, runners, backcloths, flats and wings, sound and lighting can be adequately employed without *holding up the action*, it would be pointless not to use them.

N.B. All the songs may be omitted except the finale.

Chairman Ladies and Gentlemen, we now proudly present our own potted version of Mr Douglas Jerrold's celebrated nautical drama entitled *Black-Eye'd Susan*. The setting is the naval town of Deal in Sussex, and the time is ten years after the Battle of Trafalgar. For ten years, then, this right little tight little island has ruled the waves, as she does to this very day! (*Wait for cheers to subside*) I ought to point out that several of the artistes in our company have most unfortunately been laid low by a severe attack of (*local brewery's*) gloom and are therefore unable to appear. However, Mr. *N* has kindly agreed to sustain the vacant roles, and I am convinced you will find Mr *N*'s Protean exhibitions no bar to your enjoyment of the rollicking events about to take place before your very glassy eyes.
(*Music: introduction to "Black-Eye'd Susan" by John Gay & Richard Leveridge*)
A trim little craft is our Susan of Deal;
Her husband's at sea—think how she must feel . . .

Enter Susan down L

Susan (*sings*) "All in the downs, the fleet was moored,
The streamers waving in the wind;
When Black-Eye'd Susan came on board,
'O, where shall I my true love find?
Tell me, jovial sailors, tell me true,
Does my sweet William, does my sweet William,
sail among your crew?
Tell me, jovial sailors, tell me true,
Does my sweet William, does my sweet William,
sail among your crew?' "

Susan exits sadly down R

Chairman Here's Crosstree, an officer, and I'm sorry to state:
A captain, who's desirous of Sue for his mate!

Enter Crosstree, in mufti, down L *to suitably villainous music. If there is a follow-spot, it can turn green briefly*

Crosstree Listen to my story: it shall be short—short as a marlin-spike. I will have Susan . . . I burn for that delicate little Black-Eye'd Susan. I shall tell her that her husband, William, who served aboard my ship, is drowned—she will never know that I marooned him, accidentally, of *course!*, on a South Sea island where I'd stopped to water. Her rascally old uncle, Dog-grass——

Enter Doggrass down L

—who is her landlord—
Doggrass (*indicating Crosstree*) —and *his* partner——
Crosstree —will demand his arrears of rent, seize her goods, and turn her adrift. I shall pay her debts, leaving her no chance but to marry me in duty and gratitude. Is it not a good scheme?
Doggrass Ay, that it is, Captain—especially the bit about seizing my niece's goods . . . (*He laughs into Crosstree's face. He has bad breath, and Crosstree reacts accordingly*)

Both exeunt chuckling evilly down R

Chairman But William is nigh—he's safe and he's sound!
For Susan's soft arms his course is now bound!

(*Music: introduction to "The Girl I Left Behind Me", trad.*)

Enter William down L

William (*sings*)
"I've been so lonely since I went across the seas a-cruising,
With heavy thoughts my heart was rent,
Since parting from my Susan.
But now I never more will roam,
In Deal is where you'll find me,
Kind heaven's winds have brought me home
To the girl I left behind me!"

Reprise last 16 bars molto allegro for William to dance a hornpipe.

Exit down R

Chairman Now we have met all the chief protagonists of this salty, soggy, saga, so adjust your sou'westers, please, as we take you into Susan's rude cottage for the first of "Black-Eye'd Susan" or "Thuggery, Skulduggery, and Buccaneering!"

SCENE I

Music. Runners open to reveal interior of a humble cottage. Chair up LC. *If there are no runners, the Chairman can set the chair during the previous speech*

Susan (*entering up* R) Twelve long months have passed since last I received tidings of William. Shame upon the unkind hearts that have parted us—that have sent my dear husband to dare the perils of the ocean, and made me a miserable pining creature. Oh, the pangs! the dreadful pangs that tear the sailor's wife, as wakeful on her tear-wet pillow she lists and trembles at the roaring sea.

Doggrass (*entering up* R) Now, Susan . . .

Chord

Susan (*down* L) Uncle Doggrass! (*She curtsies*)

Doggrass You know my business. I come for money.

Susan I have none, sir.

Doggrass A pretty answer, truly. Are people to let their houses to beggars?

Susan Beggars! Sir, I am your brother's orphan child.

Doggrass I am sorry for it. I wish he were alive to pay for you. And where is Dame Hatley who lives with you?

Susan In the next room, ill. Very ill.

Doggrass Ha! An excuse to avoid me. She shall not. (*He moves to up* L)

Susan (*barring his way*) You will not enter.

Doggrass Who shall stop me?

Susan (*moving down* C *for maximum effect*) If heaven give me power—I! (*Moving back up*) Uncle, the old woman is sick—I fear dangerously. Uncle—Landlord! Would you have murder on your soul?

Doggrass Can Dame Hatley pay me the money?
Susan No.
Doggrass Then she shall go to prison.
Susan She will die there!
Doggrass Well? I have no time for sentiment. I'll take whatever may be in the house—(*he removes a picture from the wall. To his chagrin another precisely like it is painted on the scenery behind it*)—and return to fetch the rest with a tipstaff . . .
Crosstree (*entering up* R) Steady there! (*His outstretched arm smashes through the picture*)

Chord

None of your overhauling! What do you want with the young woman? (*Disentangling himself*)
Doggrass (*heavily overacting*) What's that to you? (*He winks at Crosstree*)
Susan Oh, pray don't quarrel on my account—do not, I entreat you!
Crosstree (*aside*) I'll swagger a little. (*Aloud, crossing to her*) Quarrel, my dear? I'd fight a whole squadron of Frenchies for you; go on a boarding party; row under a battery or fight in a rocket boat—anything!
Doggrass Will you pay the money she owes?
Crosstree (*airily*) How much is it?
Doggrass Twelve pounds, seventeen and sixpence.
Crosstree There's thirteen pounds—(*hands over the bag of coins*) —I'm not much of an accountant, but it strikes me that will pay your bill, and leave just a dirty little two-and-sixpence for your bumboy outside. Now, unship your moorings and luff your hulk to some other jetty!
Doggrass With pleasure, Captain. With pleasure. (*With more winks he goes out up* R)
Susan Oh, my good kind friend! My thanks! My prayers. Whatever can I do to repay you?
Crosstree (*aside*) Steady, Crosstree, steady . . .
Susan This generosity—and from a stranger.
Crosstree Not such a stranger as you may think. Your husband sailed under my command.
Susan You—his captain! Where is he? Oh, tell me everything!

Crosstree Susan, you must prepare to be brave. . . . Sit you down, my dear.
Susan Oh . . . ! (*Sitting up* L)

Lights fade as Crosstree begins to tell Susan his wicked lies; or runners in; or Crosstree and Susan freeze

SCENE II

The quayside (front cloth)

Music—"The Girl I Left Behind Me" as William and Seaweed enter down R

William (*swaying as though still on deck*) Huzza, huzza! Seaweed, my old shipmate, my head turns round like a capstan to be back on dear old England's shore again! Had it not been for your sharp eyes in the topmast of the *Arethusa* I might still be rotting on that heathen island.
Seaweed (*also swaying*) Sure, 'twas providence I was on watch that morn, sure 'twas—you was nearly a gonner, sure an' bejasus you was. (*Both stop swaying*)
William And we've been good messmates ever since. (*They shake hands manfully*)
Seaweed Ah'm away the noo fur a wee droppie at yon hostelry. Hoo aboot yoo, Wullie?
William Not this time, my *Irish* friend . . .
Seaweed (*sotto voce*) Oh . . .
William It's full sail and a straight course for my haven of joy. Call on us at six bells, Seaweed, and you'll meet my own dear little cutter!
Seaweed Indeet ant I'll do that, Will-yum bach! Begorrah . . .

Seaweed exits down R

William Three years before the mast, and all that time dreaming of Susan. For three years walking the deck with the surf beating in my face, but Susan was at my side and I did not feel it . . . in battle I saw my shipmates lying torn and mangled about me—I'd whisper "Susan", a word that kept me safe as it turned the balls aside . . . I'd grip my weapon and plunge into the fray again . . . then alone on that scurvy island all those weeks—how did Cap'n Crosstree come to leave me behind? He must have sighted an enemy flotilla and sailed into action. Aye, that'll be it: duty must come first! (*This should raise cheers from the audience*) And now I am here at last! I've swallowed the anchor, so:

Arpeggio from piano

Sings to the last 8 bars of "The Girl I Left Behind Me"

"No foreign maidens fine or gay can do but to remind me
How swift the hours did pass away with the girl I left behind me."

William exits down R, *hornpiping*

SCENE III

The cottage again

Susan (*sitting up* L) Oh, say not so. Is there no hope?

Crosstree Hope? None, I tell you, Susan. Our ship got upon rocks, her timbers opened and I gave orders to take to the boats. William was in the jolly-boat; she hadn't got the length of a boarding-pike when she shipped a sea and down she went. William and twelve other brave fellows were in the water—I threw him a rope, but it was too late. William sank and was never seen any more.

Enter William, unperceived, up R

Susan (*weeping*) Oh, these are heavy tidings indeed . . .

William (*aside*) What's this? 'Tis she! Hanging out signals of distress . . . and with a strange-rigged craft in convoy.

Crosstree (*with his back to William*) Don't take on so, sweet Susan. If William is dead, there are husbands enough for so pretty a face.

William (*aside*) Dead? I'll be pooped—if that swab don't want to climb into my hammock!

Crosstree Come, Sue, let me comfort you . . . (*He attempts to embrace her*)

William Now he's rowing alongside with muffled oars . . . I'll cut his rigging for him! (*Aloud*) Avast there, you bilge rat! Belay your grappling irons! (*He draws his cutlass and strikes Crosstree with the flat of the blade. Crosstree turns with both hands across his face to protect himself*)

Susan William!

William belabours Crosstree who makes his way to the up R *exit. As he backs out William thrusts and wounds him*

William There! Go and scupper yourself! (*He turns and takes Susan in his arms*)

Crosstree I deserve me fate!

Crosstree exits up R

Susan Oh, William, I thought you were lost! I thought we should never meet again!

William Not meet? Why, we shall never part again—my captain promised to write to the Admiralty for my discharge. (*Straight to the audience*) I saved his life in the Basque Roads. But what's this? (*Looking around*) Poverty aboard?

Susan Oh, William—my uncle was about to turn us out—why, Uncle!

Doggrass (*entering with his hand out, up* R) William, my boy . . .

William (*ignoring the hand*) Avast, there! Don't think to come under my lee in that fashion. Aren't you a neat lubber of an uncle now, to cut the painter of a pretty pinnace like this and send her adrift without ballast, provision or compass?

Doggrass William, the marines are here to take you into custody!

A musket barrel appears up R

William Me? In the brig? Why? For why?

Susan William—that man who was here: it was—Captain Crosstree!

William Crosstree! My captain!

Doggrass Yes, I thought that would take the wind out of your sails, you young hot-head. Your captain—you gave him a nasty gash in the shoulder. Striking a superior officer—it's the yard-arm for you, my fine spunky lad! The yard-arm!

Doggrass exits cackling up R

William Keel-hauled! I've dropped anchor for the last time, it seems.
Susan And I have watched and prayed for your return; smiled in the face of poverty; without friends, except for Dame Hatley . . .
William How is she?
Susan Sick.
William Oh.

These last three lines to be said very quickly

Susan And for what? For this . . . (*She clings to him*)
William Aye, Susan, it's hard; but I might have died disgraced—have left you at the mercy of a bad, black-hearted man; now I know 'twill not be so, and in this at least there is some comfort—(*moving down* C)—that I die in defence of the virtue of a wife! (*He waits for cheers*)

Enter Marine holding the musket which has been in sight all the time. He walks behind William and marches him off

Susan (*weeping*) Oh, William . . .

Susan exits up L, *taking a chair with her. Black-Out*

Scene IV

The Admiral's Cabin

A small podium, twelve inches square and six inches in height is up C. *A light picks out the Chairman seated down* L

Chairman (*half-dressed as admiral with large epaulettes, an ad-*

miral's hat and an eye-patch) Prisoner, you are charged with an attempt to slay Robert Crosstree, Captain of his Majesty's Navy, and your superior officer, who is still too grievously wounded to attend this court martial. Answer, are you guilty or not guilty?

A light picks out William, standing just below the podium

William If it be guilt to strike in defence of a sailor's own sheet-anchor, his wife, why I say "guilty", your Honour; I say it, and think I've no cause to strike my colours.
Chairman Do none of your shipmates attend to speak to your character?

Lights full up. Enter Quid down R *with a strong limp and wearing large ear-rings and a hat*

Quid (*heavy Jewish accent*) There's me, your Honour.
Chairman What are you?
Quid Quid, the bo'sun, your Honour.
Chairman What know you of the prisoner?
Quid Know, your Honour? (*Laughing*) My life! The trimmest sailor as ever handled rope; the first on his watch, the last to leave the deck; from reefing a main top'sle to stowing a netting, give me taut Bill afore any able seaman in his Majesty's fleet, already.
Chairman Very well. You may stand down.
Quid (*knuckling his forehead*) Aye, aye, sir. (*Going*) Poor Bill—oi vay . . . !

Quid exits down R

Chairman Are there any other witnesses?
Pike (*off* R) Aye!

Pause

Chairman (*looking off worriedly*) Are there any other witnesses?

Pike enters down R. *He has not hat or ear-rings or limp, but he does have a large false beard*

Pike Aye, there's me, your Honour. Ordinary Seaman Pike. (*Strong Lancashire*)
Chairman What do you know of the prisoner.
Pike Nowt but good, your Honour.
Chairman He was never known to disobey a command?
Pike Nobbut once, your Honour, and that was when he gave me half his grog ration when ah was on t'black list.
Chairman And what else do you know?
Pike Why this, your Honour—if William has to swing, theere's promotion for 'im oop yonder . . . (*Gesturing to the heavens*)
Chairman Stand down.
Pike Aye, raight . . .

Pike exits down R

Chairman Are there any other witnesses?
Pike (*off* R) Strewth! (*In very posh accent*) No more witnesses, sir. (*This said with just his face showing wearing a pair of spectacles*)
Chairman Very well. Prisoner, what have you to say in arrest of judgement? Now is your time to speak.
William (*coming down* C) Your Honour, three years ago I left my wife—as sweet a little craft as was ever larnched, and with cheeks as rosy as the King's head on the side of a fire-bucket—and all that time never looked upon or heard from her. So when I came ashore I was as lively as a petrel, but . . .
Chairman (*involuntarily*) As a what?
William (*annoyed at having his big speech spoiled*) A petrel.
Chairman (*still puzzled*) Oh . . . carry on.
William But then, when I drew alongside our little cabin, I found Susan—that's my wife, your Honour—about to be boarded by some pirate vessel. I out with my cutlass, made all sail, and came up under his stern. I never looked at his figure-head—would you, your Honour?
Chairman Well . . .
William (*furious at again being interrupted*) No! No, you wouldn't! For the gilt swabs on your shoulder can't alter the heart that swells beneath; you would have done as I did—and what did I? Why, I cut him down like a piece of old junk—had he been First Lord of the Admiralty, I had done it! (*He is overcome. Wait for cheers*)

Chairman Have you anything further to advance?
William All my cable is run out—I'm brought to.
Chairman Prisoner, keenly as I feel for your situation, it is now my most painful duty to pass the sentence of this Court upon you. Your case falls under the twenty-second Article of War. (*He picks up a large book and holds it under his patched eye, then moves it round till he can read*) "If any man in, or belonging to, the Fleet, shall draw or offer to draw or lift up his hand against his superior officer, he shall suffer death." (*He puts the book down*) The sentence of the Court is that you be hanged at the fore-yard-arm of this His Majesty's Ship at the hour of ten o'clock. Heaven pardon your sins, and have mercy on your soul. (*He bangs the gavel*) Guard!

Enter Marine up R *who salutes ostentatiously with his musket*

This Court is dismissed.

Exit Marine up R, *deflated and muttering*

The lights fade leaving only the centre stage illuminated

Enter Susan up L

Susan Oh, William . . . (*Weeping bitterly*)
William (*heroically calm*) Susan, be calm.
Susan Oh, oh, oh . . . (*Crying noisily*)
William (*with a touch of asperity—his big moment is being ruined again*) Susan, be calm.
Susan Oh William . . . (*Still blubbing loudly*)
William (*in a fierce whisper*) Shut up! (*Recovering himself*) Susan, if you love your husband, do not send him on the deck a white-faced coward. Think only that I am a-sailing on a long foreign station. Come, my poor wench, have you nothing to say to me?
Susan Oh, husband—here is good Dame Hatley to bid you . . . farewell!

Enter Dame Hatley down R *in loose floor-length dress and with shawl over "her" head. "She" goes to William and kisses him*

William Farewell, Dame Hatley. After I'm gone, keep convoy with my little pinnace.

Dame Hatley nods and turns to hobble off down R. *Inadvertently dropping the musket from under "her" voluminous skirts. "She" picks it up hurriedly and exits in confusion down* R

Now, my own Sue. Let us lock bow-sprits for the last time.

They embrace and Susan exits up L *in floods of tears*

SCENE V

The quarter-deck

A drum is heard beating slowly off stage; William mounts the rostrum and a noose descends from the flies above his head as the lights come up and ratlines appear to suggest the deck of a sailing-ship. Susan re-enters up L, *the Marine beating his drum with one hand and holding his musket with the other appears up* R. *The Admiral rises and steps forward a pace. The Marine stops beating but a drum in the wings continues for two more beats*

Marine (*Ulster accent*) Prisoner, are you prepared?

William (*his finest moment*) Bless you! Bless you all! I fear not death: in the storm I have heeded him not—in the fury of the battle I've looked upon his face and shrunk not. Of me let it be said: *he did his duty!!!* (*Wait for cheers from audience*)

Chairman Carry out the sentence.

Susan Oh!

Marine (*Cockney accent*) Right y'are, guv. (*He struggles with drum and musket trying to reach the noose. Eventually William surreptitiously holds the musket while the noose is placed around his neck*)

Crosstree (*off*) Hold! Hold! Admiral, sir, hold!

Captain Crosstree enters hurriedly down R *with his arm in a sling*

Admiral Captain Crosstree, retire!

Crosstree Never! If the prisoner be executed, he is a murdered man. I alone am the culprit—'twas I who would have dishonoured him.

Chairman This cannot plead here—he struck a superior officer.

Crosstree No!

Omnes No?

Crosstree He saved my life in the Basque Roads! I . . .

Chairman (*involuntarily*) In the where?

Crosstree (*his big moment spoiled, too*) In the Basque Roads!

Chairman (*softly*) Oh . . . (*Obviously uncomprehending*)

Crosstree I had written for his discharge. Villainy has kept back the document—'tis here dated back. (*He hands the paper to the Admiral*) When William struck me he was not the King's sailor —I was not his officer!

Chairman (*reads; same business with eye-patch*) He is free!

Omnes cheer. William takes off the noose. Susan runs to him and they embrace. The Marine disencumbers himself of his drum and musket

Omnes (*singing*) "Rule Britannia! Britannia rules the waves!
Britons never, never, never shall be slaves!"

During this a Union Flag flies in

Lights snap down to illuminate Susan only

Susan (*singing to last 8 bars of "Black-Eye'd Susan*)
"Tell me, ladies and gentlemen, tell me do;
Will my sweet William,
Will my sweet William,
Always love me true?"

William (*singing to same music*)
"Yes, my dear, my little turtle-dove,
My little Susan,
My Black-Eye'd Susan,
Never doubt my love! For—

Lights snap up full

To last 8 bars of "The Girl I Left Behind Me"

Now I never more will roam
In Deal is where you'll find me,
For Captain Crosstree's sent me home,

To the girl I left behind me."
Omnes (*singing*) "Yes, Captain Crosstree's sent him home,
To the girl he left behind he!"

To last 8 bars of "The Girl I left Behind Me"

"And now our tale is ended right
And we've reached our conclusion;
William Remember honour and the King.
Omnes And William and his Susan!
Remember honour and the King
And William and his Susan!"

CURTAIN

FIRST TABLEAU: *Marine has hand on Crosstree's shoulder in attitude of arrest; William has one arm round Susan and with the other is shaking the Admiral's hand.*

SECOND TABLEAU: *William has Susan on the other arm and is being kissed by Dame Hatley;*[1] *Crosstree is standing with head bowed in front of angry Admiral.*

THIRD TABLEAU: *Straightforward line-up and bows.*

Chairman (*removing his hat, epaulettes and eye-patch*) Ah, dear me, that William reminds me of my youth . . . I think *he* joined the Navy . . . but I've always had a hankering for a life at sea, myself. It must be wonderful—all those rowlocks and bollards and things . . .

[1] This startlingly quick change may be achieved by cheating—the person wearing the Dame Hatley costume being someone other than the Marine.

FURNITURE AND PROPERTY LIST

On stage throughout Set A Thief To Catch A Thief and *The Bells:* Chairman's table down R; for *Black-Eye'd Susan* the Chairman's table is presumed to be down L.

SET A THIEF TO CATCH A THIEF

On stage: A table up C

Off stage: (L) Box or beer crate, chair, calico strip or velcro, baby

Personal: 2 bottles of beer **(Alf)**
Loaded revolver **(Alf)**
Packet of cigarettes **(Alf)**
Bottle-opener on string **(Charlie)**
Box of matches **(Charlie)**
(L) Wallet containing pound notes **(Peter)**

THE BELLS

On stage: Nil

Off stage: (*Down* R) 3 milk bottles, motor horn, rattle, swanee whistle, sleigh bells, axe, saucepan and spoon
(*Up* L) Bucket of snow, Powder for lime kiln

Personal: (L) Hat-box containing hat **(Mathias)**
(L) Cue-sheet
Cigar and matches
Rope 4 ft. 6 in. long
} **(Stage-Manager)**

BLACK-EYE'D SUSAN

On stage: Scene I Chair up LC
Portrait on wall

Scene II Nil

Scene III Chair up LC

Scene IV Nil

Scene V Box or small rostrum up C (Set off stage up R)
Drum and stick

Personal: (R) Bag of coins (**Crosstree**)
(R) Musket (**Marine**)
(R) Spectacles
Large book (Articles of War) on Chairman's table (*down* L)
(R) Drum and stick (**Marine**)
(R) Sling, discharge paper (**Crosstree**)

LIGHTING PLOT

In addition to the general lighting, suitably coloured following-spots should be used for the various characters. (Pink for the girls, straw or amber for the men)

SET A THIEF TO CATCH A THIEF

A humble living-room

General lighting throughout

Cue 1 **Alf:** "... but your rhubarb must be forced!" (Page 12)
Black-out, then up to full

Cue 2 **Alf:** "... Oh, no, you won't!" (*Gunshot*) (Page 13)

Black-out, then up to full for Chairman. No calls

THE BELLS

Interior of an inn in Alsace

To open: General lighting

Cue 1 **Chairman:** "... Mr Leopold Lewis's famed drama: *The Bells*!" (Page 17)
Lights lower

Cue 2 Mathias's entrance (Page 19)
Lights up to full

Cue 3 **Mathias:** "Thank 'ee, thank 'ee, my boy." (Page 19)
Walks out of following-spot. He walks back into the spot pointedly and this time it follows him

Cue 4 Exit **Ann** and **Christian** (Page 20)
Lights lower

Cue 5	**Mathias:** "... the moon shines its frosty radiance on the scene." *Brief black-out. Lights up then a blue filter is slowly and noisily pushed either into the following-spot or a flood in the wings*	(Page 22)
Cue 6	**Mathias:** ". . . into the lime kiln." (Mimes opening oven door) *Red spot comes on up* L	(Page 22)
Cue 7	Mathias mimes shutting kiln door *Red spot out*	(Page 22)
Cue 8	**Stage-Manager:** ". . . righto, my son. Anything to oblige." (He garrots Mathias) *Black-out, then up to full for Chairman. No calls*	(Page 23)

BLACK-EYE'D SUSAN

Prologue

To open: General lighting

Scene 1. Cottage interior: General lighting

Cue 1	**Crosstree:** "Susan, you must prepare to be brave . . ." *Quick fade to black-out. Then up to full*	(Page 32)

Scene II. Front Cloth: General lighting

Scene III. Cottage interior: General lighting

Cue 2	**William:** "Aye, Susan, it's hard . . ." *Lights begin to lower*	(Page 35)
Cue 3	**William** exits with **Marine.** **Susan:** "Oh, William . . ." *Fade to black-out*	(Page 35)

Scene IV. The Court Martial

Cue 4	(Immediately after the previous black-out) *Spot picks out* **Chairman** *as* **Admiral** *down* L	(Page 35)

Cue 5 **Chairman:** ". . . are you guilty or not guilty?" (Page 36)
Bring up spot on **William** C

Cue 6 **Chairman:** "Do none of your shipmates attend to speak to your character?" (Page 36)
Bring up spot on **Quid** *down* R

Cue 7 **Chairman:** "This Court is dismissed." (Page 38)
Exit **Marine**
Fade out all lights except spot on William

Cue 8 **William:** "Let us lock bowsprits for the last time." Exit **Susan** (Page 39)

Fade general lighting up to ¾ Early morning

Scene V. The deck

Cue 9 **Omnes** (*singing*): "Rule Britannia . . ." (Page 40)
General lighting up to full

Cue 10 **Omnes** (*singing*) ". . . shall be slaves . . ." (Page 40)
Snap down to single spot on Susan down C

Cue 11 **William** (*singing*): ". . . never doubt, my love. For . . ." (Page 40)
Snap up general lighting to full

Cue 12 As runners come in and out for calls, *fade F.O.H. down and up.* If there are no runners or house-tabs available, the following cue will apply instead: (Page 41)

Omnes (*singing*): ". . . and William and his Susan!" (Second time) (Page 41)

Black-out. Up to full for first tableau, then black-out. Up to full for second tableau, then black-out. Then as needed for straight line-ups. Then up to full for **Chairman**

EFFECTS PLOT

SET A THIEF TO CATCH A THIEF

Cue 1 **Chairman:** "Have we a box, please?" (Page 4)
A box or beer crate is hurled on from down L

Cue 2 **Chairman:** "Three chairs, please!" (Second time) (Page 5)
A chair is hurled on from down L
(These two cues do not apply if the **Stage-Manager** enters)

Cue 3 **Alf:** "Or on his pot." (Page 7)
Knock on door L
"There's someone at the door".
More knocks
"I said there's someone at the door."
Yet more knocks

Cue 4 **Peter:** "The police are after me." (Page 9)
Heavy footsteps off L

Cue 5 **Inspector Hawkshaw:** "There is no way out." (Page 10)
Calico rip off (or Velcro)

THE BELLS

Cue 1 **Stage-Manager:** "Don't you worry about me... My life!" (Exit) (Page 17)
Chink of milk bottles down L

Cue 2 Enter **Ann** (Page 18)
Loud wind
She shuts the door.
Wind cuts off sharply

Cue 3 **Ann:** "Hark—a footfall!" (Enter **Christian**) (Page 18)
Loud wind

He shuts the door
Wind cuts off sharply

Cue 4	Enter **Mathias** *Loud wind*	(Page 19)
Cue 5	**Mathias:** "What a snowstorm!" *Snow thrown over Mathias up* L	(Page 19)
Cue 6	**Mathias:** "I'll shut the door!" *Wind cuts off sharply*	(Page 19)
Cue 7	**Stage-Manager:** "Morrie! Give us the bells." *Motor horn, rattle, swanee whistle, one after the down* L	(Page 20)
Cue 8	**Stage-Manager:** "All right, all right . . ." *Clink of milk bottles down* L "Ah, here we are." *Sleigh bells down* L	(Page 20)
Cue 9	**Mathias:** "What is this jangling in my ears?" *Sleigh bells down* L	(Page 20)
Cue 10	**Mathias:** "Ooh, what a dreadful silence . . ." *Chink of milk bottles down* L	(Page 21)
Cue 11	**Mathias:** "Three o'clock strikes . . ." *Three beats of a spoon on a saucepan down* L "And . . ." *Another beat*	(Page 22)
Cue 12	**Stage-Manager:** "He wants that bell again, Morrie!" *Hooter, rattle, down* L "No, son—the bells! The bleeding bells!" *Sleigh bells down* L	(Page 22)
Cue 13	**Mathias:** "I have you now, Jew! I have you now!" *Thud of axe down* L	(Page 22)
Cue 14	**Mathias:** "Into the lime kiln . . ." (Mimes opening oven door) *Cloud of dust blows over* **Mathias**	(Page 22)

BLACK-EYE'D SUSAN

Cue 1 **Chairman:** ". . . before your very glassy eyes . . ." (Page 28)
Runners open to disclose front cloth. (If no cloth, cut this cue)

Cue 2 **Chairman:** ". . . thuggery, skulduggery and buccaneering." (Page 30)

Take out cloth. (If no cloth, open runners. If neither, cut this cue)

Cue 3 End of Scene I. Lights fade to black-out (Page 32)
Drop in front cloth or pull in runners

Cue 4 End of Scene II. **William** exits, hornpiping (Page 33)
Take out cloth or open runners

Cue 5 **Doggrass:** "The Marines are here to take you into custody." (Page 34)
Musket barrel appears up R

Cue 6 Start of Scene V (Page 39)

Let in noose to just above **William**'*s head. Also let in ratlines or anything which suggest the quarter-deck of a ship*

Cue 7 **Chairman:** "Carry out the sentence!" (Page 39)
Lower noose

Cue 8 **Chairman:** "He is free!" (Page 40)
Take out noose after William has been released

Cue 9 **Omnes** sing "Rule Britannia!" (Page 40)
Fly in Union Flags

Cue 10 **Omnes** sing "Remember Honour and the King, and William and his Susan" (second time) (Page 41)

Runners in. Open for the first tableau: close. Open for second tableau: close. Then open for straight line-ups as needed

N.B. If no runners or front-cloth are available, cut Cues 1 to 4 inclusive and Cue 10. The end of the finale and the calls can be indicated by black-outs instead.

COSTUMES

SET A THIEF TO CATCH A THIEF

Alf: Brown or black bowler hat, scruffy trousers (corduroy) and boots, coloured waistcoat, striped collarless shirt and choker. Heavy belt.

Charlie: Tight period suit, boots, flat cap. White shirt, wing collar, bow tie.

Polly: Gingham ¾-length dress with matching bow in hair; white tights, button or lace-up boots.

Peter: Knickerbocker suit, brown socks and shoes. (Or white trousers and striped blazer with two-tone shoes.) White shirt with rounded starched collar. Straw boater with band to match his college tie.

Hawkshaw: As Chairman plus top hat and cloak.

Uncle Silas: Grey topper, frock coat, grey waistcoat, striped or grey check trousers. Black shoes and socks. Watch-chain in waistcoat, grey gloves, ebony stick. White shirt, wing collar, grey tie or cravat with pearl tie-pin.

Stage-Manager: Black bowler hat, loud check trousers, black boots, fawn "stock-room" coat, wing-collar and bow tie.

THE BELLS

Ann: Peasant-girl's ¾-length dress with flounced petticoat, embroidered blouse with full sleeves, coloured bodice; flowers in hair; white stockings and button-boots.

Christian: Period suit (central European); wing collar and sober bow tie; boots, fur hat, gloves and fur overcoat. The gloves, hat and overcoat can be removed for the second entrance.

Mathias: *1st entrance.* Long silk dressing-gown over costume, cravat. *2nd entrance.* Wide-brimmed velour hat, cloak, Russian-type blouse over trousers; belt; knee-breeches and boots. No gloves.

Stage-Manager: Brown "foreman" coat, black boots, corduroy trousers, striped collarless shirt and choker, bowler hat.

BLACK-EYE'D SUSAN

Crosstree: Fashionable gentleman's period walking outfit (late (Regency). *Not* naval unform.

Susan: ¾-length striped cotton dress, brightly coloured, with flared petticoats. White stockings and button boots. Ribbons in the hair.

William: Matelot's uniform of the period (1828) plus cutlass.

Chairman: Admiral's hat and epaulettes.

Doggrass: Knee breeches and stockings, frilled shirt with cravat, long waistcoat and period top hat. Black buckle shoes.

Seaweed: White bell-bottoms worn over Doggrass's breeches; red and white horizontally-striped vest (worn *under* Doggrass's shirt); matelot's jacket and hat.

Marine: Remove bell-bottoms and change to period Marine's hat and long coat.

Quid: As for Seaweed plus large ear-rings (curtain-rings on string loops)

Pike: As for Seaweed, minus ear-rings but with large false beard.

Dame Hatley: Voluminous dress and shawl, or full-length cloak and hood.

MAKE-UP

SET A THIEF TO CATCH A THIEF

Alf: Thick eyebrows and small "Hitler" moustache; ruddy complexion (Leichner 5 and 4, plus a little lake); gently carmined nose.

Charlie: Chalk-white base; arched eyebrows; a single dark-brown dot above and below each eye.

Polly: Straight. Easy on the eye-shadow.

Peter: Straight; clean-shaven; hair parted in the middle.

Hawkshaw: Straight plus villainous black moustache and bushy black eyebrows.

Uncle Silas: Straight; greying hair; grey Lord Kitchener moustache; monocle or pince-nez.

THE BELLS

Ann: Rather overdone "Juv" with hectic red cheeks and extremely long false eyelashes. Hair braided in "ear-muffs".

Christian: Rather pale, hair parted in the middle; an obviously false and very unsuitable moustache to make him look older. Steel rimmed spectacles.

Mathias: Pale and gaunt, haunted; achieved with a little cigarette ash in the hollows of the cheeks and a dab of lake under the eyes. Clean shaven. Long grey hair worn without a parting. Pince-nez to be worn only for the first entrance.

Stage-Manager: Ruddy complexion, ragged grey moustache.

BLACK-EYE'D SUSAN

Crosstree: Swarthy complexion with heavy eyebrows; clean shaven; sideburns.

Susan: Straight—easy on the eye-shadow.

William: Tanned and healthy looking; clean-shaven; sideburns; pig-tail.

Doggrass: Straight plus grey sideburns.
Seaweed: Straight plus pigtail attached to hat.
Marine: Straight plus large black moustache.
Quid: Straight plus ear-rings. No Hat (Limp)
Pike: Straight plus large false beard—ginger.
Dame Hatley: Marine's large black moustache.
Chairman: Eye-patch.

BLACK - EYED SUSAN.

CUE: "BEFORE YOUR VERY GLASSY EYES"

ANDANTE.

SUSAN

ALL IN THE DOWNS, THE FLEET WAS

MOORED, THE STREAMERS
WA-WING IN THE
WIND, WHEN BLACK-EYED
SU - SAN CAME ON
BOARD, OH WHERE SHALL

I MY TRUE LOVE
FIND? TELL ME
JOVIAL SAILORS TELL ME
TRUE, DOES MY SWEET

WILLIAM, DOES MY SWEET
WILLIAM, SAIL A-
MONG YOUR
CREW? TELL ME
JOVIAL SAILORS TELL ME

TRUE, DOES MY SWEET
WILLIAM DOES MY SWEET
WILLIAM SAIL A-
MONG YOUR
CREW?

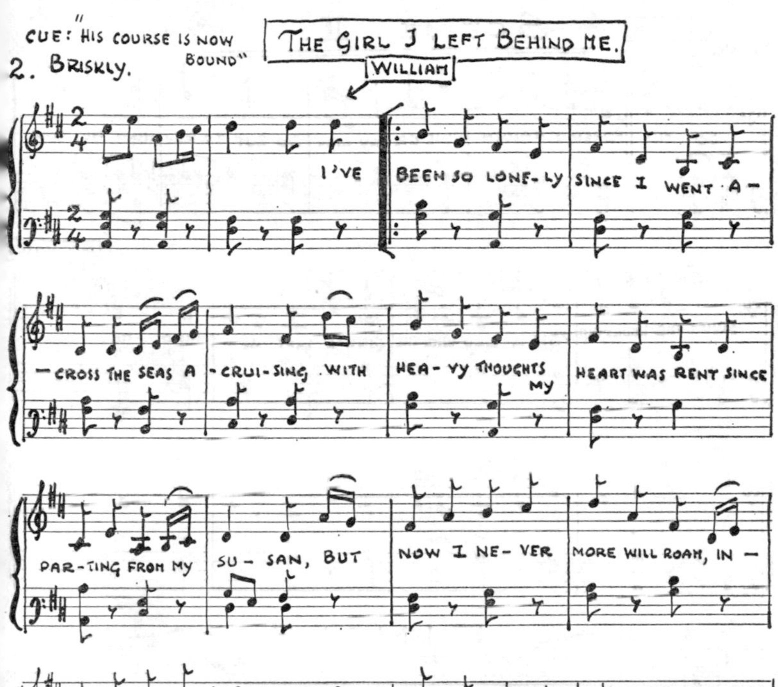
CUE: "HIS COURSE IS NOW BOUND"
2. BRISKLY.
THE GIRL I LEFT BEHIND ME.
WILLIAM
I'VE
BEEN SO LONE-LY
SINCE I WENT A-
-CROSS THE SEAS A
-CRUI-SING WITH
HEA-VY THOUGHTS MY
HEART WAS RENT SINCE
PAR-TING FROM MY
SU-SAN, BUT
NOW I NE-VER
MORE WILL ROAM, IN-

DEAL IS WHERE YOU'LL FIND ME, KIND
HEAVENS WINDS HAVE
BROUGHT ME HOME TO THE

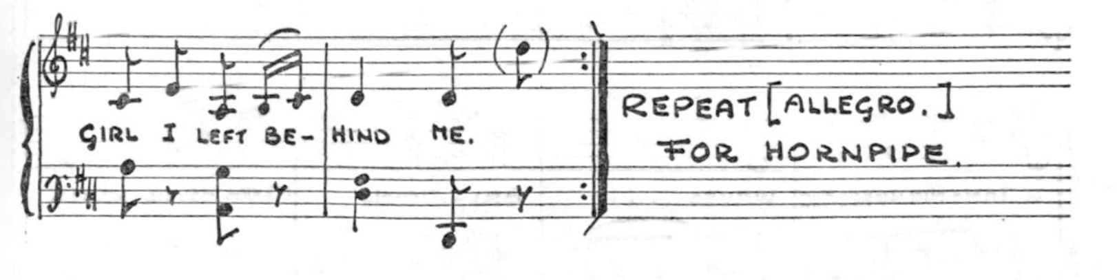
GIRL I LEFT BE-
HIND ME.
REPEAT [ALLEGRO.]
FOR HORNPIPE.

WILLIAM
SCENE. II.
BRISKLY.
SO NO FOREIGN MAIDEN FINE OR GAY CAN DO BUT TO RE- MIND ME, HOW
NO VOICE
SWIFT THE HOURS DID PASS A-WAY WITH THE GIRL I LEFT BE- HIND ME.
FINALE.
CUE: "HE IS FREE"
MARCIA
ALL
ff
RULE BRI- TAN-NIA BRI-
- TAN-NIA RULES THE WAVES .....
BRI- TAINS NEVER NEVER NEVER
B.E. SUSAN (3)

SUSAN
SHALL BE.
SLAVES. TELL ME LADIES & GENTLEMEN TELL ME DO, WILL MY SWEET
WILLIAM WILL MY SWEET WILLIAM AL-WAYS LOVE ME TRUE?
WILLIAM
YES, MY DEAR, MY LITTLE TURTLE DOVE, MY LIT-TLE SU-SAN MY BLACK-EYED SUS-AN NE-VER DOUBT MY LOVE!
FOR NOW I NEV-ER HOME WILL ROAM IN DEAL, IS WHERE YOU'LL FIND ME!
ALL
YES CAPTAIN CROSSTREE'S SENT HIM HOME TO THE GIRL HE LEFT BE-HIND ME!
MARCATO
AND NOW OUR TALE IS ENDED RIGHT AND WE'VE

WILLIAM
ALL
REA-CHED OUR CON- CLU-SION, RE- MEM-BER HON-OUR AND THE KING. AND

Deliberato.
VOICES ONLY
WILL-IAM AND HIS SU-SAN RE- MEM-BER HONOUR AND THE KING. AND

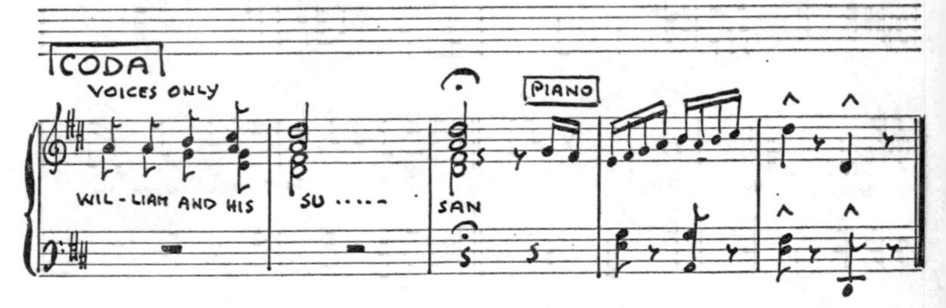
CODA
VOICES ONLY
PIANO
WIL-LIAM AND HIS SU..... SAN

FINE.